Business obesity

Gymnastics to shed the fat
Vashisht Kaushik

Fat is no fit

- Company is not just people, cash, machines and products but something less than a common pool and more than that of challenges
- Failure adds to the inertia of cultural overdose, Technological inundation, investment hysteria and excessive competition as indicators of oversized company.

Fat is fine

- Good employees numbers should be indicative of business profitability, Customer acceptance, task pipeline and stable programs of business and rival coexistence

Fat is

- Feigned àgility transition
- Future admitting threat
- Futile attempt through
- First àgility thwarted
- Failure administration team
- Fear attached tightly

Natural capital

- Customer is in need and you are getting ready to make it
- Resources are lined up with your business output in clear thought
- Goodwill and investment continue through business flows to get natural capital management.

Name the business

- IBM had to work for growth into future Behemoth unlike other companies with slimmer names.
- Size is more of your business technology - determined
- Have a clear process passport to get new geographic expansion instead of business bulking

Nutrition for business

- All employees are bound to common Business ethics
- Stakeholders are tied up with your promises to customers
- Customer is freely communicating with you
- Quality is built on best standards to Technology and Practices.

Weak and fat Business

- There's no àgility in fast momentum of Customer availability due to which you lose out on competition
- Future challenges envelop vulnerability unless we work lean and strong triggers for new business fit.

What not

- Heavy infrastructure
- Tough complex bureaucracy
- Square policy but not efficiency
- No value recognition
- Excessive financial planning

I'll do

- Prune resources to understand better and exact
- Arrangements for the future business corrections as desired by Customer commitment
- Dedication to be known for destruction of business wastes

When is fat fit?

- We don't feel comfortable with that volatility of market that is too inherent in larger dillydallying of Customer
- Education and job at loggerheads is a cause of maintaining the best range of offering and knowledge.

Fat is business failure

- Underutilized capabilities and capacity could be factors of hindrances of business success
- Promising more than most allowed excess could be a part of business obesity
- Over dominance or exaggerated communication is not just fat but some others attribute to lack of tailoring.

Fat is business value!

- Strong and healthy business relations come from nowhere but internal growth and employee numbers
- Trust in business comes with strategic Customer collaboration

Concomitant fat

- Past tracks simulating technology corrections but only for procrastination and Customer demand for forcibly competing in business etiquette rather than business relationship between products and services failure.

Occasions of business obesity

- Unclear and changing Customer segment
- Confused management policies
- Confidential program that goes along open
- Lack of communication on Innovation

But Technology is no fat

- Business growth occurs in both sides of Technological independence and acceptable human capital accumulation in the global process of establishing the business ties but some changes ought to be explored by machine learning to use less manpower.

Cultural overdose

- Belief in trouble rather than Customer
- Superstitious support without inhibiting or growing Customer doubt or participation
- Building business changes but not sure how to use that for Customer importance

Technology inundation

- Stop, test, start and change your business inclinations that credit Customer inclusion , interaction and intelligence
- Train more than needed but not without chronological market upgrading.
- Don't worry about using all technology means.

Investment hysteria

- Buy lowest, sell highest
- Invest to divest
- The goal of this investment is not a big bang profit by one time booming of business finance from start

Knowledge bank

- Knowledge prunes and not bulges to understand that space but without disturbing trends in guarantee of Customer good
- Resources change and knowledge too but only incremental unlike exclusive resources

Excessive competition

- Oligarchy rules
- Monopoly cartelises
- Higher volume of selection
- Lower division of business changes

Demand for supply

- It's better to have the same demand to exhaust your supply
- Such equilibrium is Customer pull to get your supply drive that market demand for reducing or rising by adjusting with your production supply.
- A different type of capitalism is not far away.

Supply along demand

- Customer spends and is a decision maker driving your business capabilities and supplies to get new demand patterns altering the business capacities and social change at low risk and high cost of business tardiness or low cost of business readiness to be reached by the customer networks.

New forms of capitalism

- The business that provides order of equilibrium is in the industry to be clean profit sharing model as capitalism in favour of Customer, fair gains, asset of wealth accumulation, economic precision, trade matching and growth conditions with technology dominance

Multi phony

- Product reviews
- Customer experience
- Chanñel partners' feedback
- All sorts of foul and fair sounds can be signals of business pace.

Timely response

- Too fast, too slow and too much, too low are risky for your business credibility and can impact future by improving or failing Customer loyalty and sustenance

Cut the fats

- By limiting the facts of business and competitive strategy
- The exercise of gaining weight of results from resources without any cost quantification on either side is fatty.

Fastrack business

- Understand the importance of Customer and irrelevance of business without creating Customer trust
- Thin down the wastages and other garbage activities with no value recognition
- Do not hesitate to complete the tracking within 2-3 days every semi quarter.

Gutsy management

- Dare the business teams to leave their shells and think like a customer
- Save time and money for giving more of them to Customer groups
- Challenge with changes and new goals
- Train employees in unrelated areas

Reverse business fats fast

- Hire expertise instead of choosing brand and name
- Follow image given by consumer instead of business expectations

Glean business changes

- Accumulate knowledge and momentum to apply skills
- Bank of skills that is formless and stateless must be cared into modern business administration for new change management.

Business gymming

- Champion multiple change opportunities for connecting with customers and other participants in different processes of business channel partners to share tasks and reward Customer.

Business taxing

- Let Customer think about complex and new ideas and business be tired after working with customers and for giving unexpected positive response to Customer as a preparation for fulfillment of business changes with àgility.

Business tangos

- An error occurred is a reminder of your business àgility missed
- Practices that encourage multiple viewpoint analyses come from flexible stakeholders and that discomfiture of Customer hassle gets converted into easy Business dealings.

Business rants

- Heavy discussion meetings with no major new results should be avoided
- Hi frequency traveling and visits could cause confusion with customers and employees

Industry pinning

- Redundancy and ambiguity should be minimised by allowing industry checks and balances for new business solution fitment and that should be given to customer for true quality assessment.

Agility by operations

- Quick and accurate analysis, evaluation, delegation, assessment, review, rework, testing, finalisation
- Feedback and approval systems under short process cycles.

Cool down

- High end quality jumps without detailed analysis of business changes and market progression as preparation for fearless rivalries could not buy on your business credibility.

Increase your

- Business change through finite innovation
- Business chances of winning smiles on Customers
- Business ethics of Customer development

Decrease

- Dependency on single Customer, product or technology
- Risk analysis because anyway you have to do what Customer wants now or later
- Time delay in business bridging of Customer difference

Reprioritize

- Restructuring everyday is no easy
- Tasks and responsibilities have to be visited and reallocated to get a better business outcome and output as frequently as possible.

Build bridges

- Between provider and buyer community to cut off exertion of users and sellers when they differ, help, justify, understand or adjust to one another because such distance could let fat creep in business bringing down on agility.

Restrictions

- Control your company expenses
- Reduce business expectations but not buyer dreams
- Tie up new ways but not old success recipe for new pace.

Tele-visits

- Company should show how other customers and stakeholders are treated as customer motivation and attention Strategy in recorded real interaction or other dramatic recreation. That creates opportunity to customer interaction.

Live vs offline

- Understand that space in which company could convert Business into future Customer preferences by allowing advanced customisation or spontaneous personalization without falling in traps of technical formalities.

lining up with guarantee

- Assure that you want to deal with trust, delight, access, acceptance, attention, availability, growth, and not short term interest of business with customers.

Higher values

- Give one extra loyalty reason for each customer everyday
- Additional value can come from price, functions, interaction, experience, understanding

Form notifications to individuals

- Address each customer instead of a group
- Deal with impression that goes along with every user and nonusers that come across your business promotion or output.

Gain first mover slot

- By understanding well users, haters, markets
- By fighting the business weaknesses
- By inviting competitors for slime show

Begin with

- Current scenario for better future business changes with customers from rivals
- Existing users should be able to get new gains of business changes.

Begin again

- By industry standards
- Before Customer tells
- New corrections
- Old challenges and check if you learn atleast one new impact or earn another benefit

Begin later

- What could be managed better late
- When you reach pool of difference
- Where change is prominent

Use cautiously

- Technology is liable to change faster than fastest
- Customer is no averse to be a rolling stone of business grasses
- Time and market are their own kings.

Balancing user bloating

- Customer is no protected from catching up our business patterns altering their inner efficacies leading to lethargy of decision and actions putting up airs on wrong reason causing bloating occasionally of business relationship.

Fatty myths

- To have the customer silence instead of business realities, let Customer shout and blame for that's not going to shut down your business but lack or bad response therefore.

Slim tactics

- Govern your business by Customer rules
- Commit your business resources to customer goals
- Cultivate your business credibility by Customer trust

Strategic strength

- Credit your business success to the customer relationship as that goes along fatty strength of making your customers feel great about association with you on successful company Strategic planning.

True value

- The business pillars are founding charter for new business opportunity in different forms of missions of Customer value.

Limiting the reach

- Don't overdo
- Company is not a solution for all Business challenges and Customer demand but could handle any
- Don't let the milk of business changes be spilt by the cats in the global market.

Ubiquitous slimming

- Play with the accompanying technology and product innovation to get new corporate slimming of all necessary spots instead of choosing broad procedural and operational fitness.

Calculation for profit

- Today's expenses could show you results in not less than a year or two for non financial leadership advantages
- Costs, prices, interest, interaction and change can be evaluated in customer satisfaction.

Blue water

- Oceans of unexplored market get replaced by advanced pools in various business sectors that you want to understand to tap into future buyer pipelines
- Today we have a great business saturation and can turn for drought and tap drops in business failure event for poor innovation

What is business fat?

- Failure accumulates tugs of war with customers from fragmented understanding of mistakes and needs
- First adamant tussle is a full action test of business patience for Customer.

Brewing drift

- Differential distances emerge in customer and employee intentions when Customer notices hidden Business gravity logs that prevent company from making quality pace jumps.

Deliberate difference

- Some differences are mandatory for Customer space contracting with your future business outlines, and not leading to lethargy and excess wastes but only for work comfort with your risky innovation.

Shortcuts

- May fail when competitors would work hard and smart
- Forced downsizing
- Failed budget restrictions

Constant exhaustion is 'no'

- Burning out employees
- Overworked projects
- Continuous Customer harping
- Above could be harsh obstructors of abilities to be a fat , low àgility Business.

Flow steady

- Product is most agile enough space in business flow of natural Customer response
- Even while managing market excesses Companies can adopt Customer process to be working effectively in the global agile arena.

Gnawing rivals

- Buffer helps you surrender the business wastage to rivals but a foolproof sturdy Strategy is needed for full knowledge and skills conducive to corporate governance.

Business health check

- Too lean without any involvement in getting ready for Customer scenarios is unhealthy artificial fatcutting of business.
- Monitor asset management program to understand the business health.

To avoid corporate obesity

- The employees should be happy-go-lucky and not the customer alone
- The extra resources and information must be used wisely

Nothing is not no-fat

- No risk is no competition
- No expenses is no investment in customer
- No returns but no loyalty is not Business
- Above could empower company theoretically but not without loss of good practicality

Most is no fat

- More details on Customers could not but help us increase our relationship commitment by allowing resources to that effect.
- More expenses due to the initial yes then no of Customer are basis for new account experiment.

Repeating might not help

- In this world of business witchcraft and hackers as with Facebook
- In this case of failure to pay against the business lacunae as with public sector firms
- Instead of repeating fruitlessly on cost control strategy, company can repeal the global bad Practices.

Replacement of bulky Strategy

- Over concentration of business and buyer management could be replaced by advanced market research Strategy for holistic approach and implementation success.

Is not fat

- Fruition of needs of Customer, accountability in the global network, truthful communication
- Firing employees without any involvement, answering the phone call from your business customers at any time, tuning to understand that Customer without talking.

Classic fat Business

- Competition is now caring two hoots because anyway you are happy with your business lean without buffering of necessary resources against Gorilla leadership of industry standards so be ready to smile at different scale bulges.

Face the user books

- How do you think users would have your business interpreted in their books?
- You should not deter their interpretation
- Professional services that provide protection of trust care for your customers more than a cash back.

Rating that chubby department

- Marketing realities turn for your business fat on
- Interdependent units could mash in business excess
- Grill the business entity to understand the gloss behind the pinks.

Marooning Customer blues

- Draw the line of business returns but as continuous scope of strategic Customer collaboration in adjustments with thwarting Customer concerns about you as innovators in making.

Slog like a donkey

- Tomorrow is at the same global dependency on hard toil because anyway smartness is a common buzzword of Customer and Business alike, so spike up with your customer to care for them to be cared for by Customer commitment for your business services.

Learn from animals

- Dog's loyalty without fussy barking
- Cat's confidence without thankless attitude
- Horse for selfless service without blind falls
- Fishing joy without draining water
- Birds' hardwork without compromising on quality

It's OK to be afraid

- Of Customer as your culture head
- Of corrections adopted by competition
- Of lies in the global company brochures and ads

Balancing the global focus

- Single market gets blurred by advanced customisation or spontaneous expansion in adjusting with customers from different directions

Ignore the index of business changes

- Don't instigate and poke around existence of Customer as your need of each chapter of business changes unless they are not averse to be known as brand champions of business with you.

Team up with your future prospects

- Collect competitors
- Rate their customers and give them profitable promise to stay behind every successful failure of business rivals

Trust in the competitors

- They will not take any chance of losing Customer to you
- They're sure to beat your competition
- They will not come through to the toss
- Above truth never fails to warn you when Business excesses land in.

Justify less

- Talk less in front of Customer and technology but not competitors
- Accept responsibility of Customer mistakes in return for more than trust

Analogies

- Company is mangoes and Customer is leaf who can leave
- Company offering is bananas and Customer management is no peels
- Company is not different from the bark and Customer is audience.

Combine custom with customers

- Traditional Business and modern Customer
- Oldest ethics and latest knowledge
- New technology and old questions
- Above could empower Customer with results based on culture Innovation.

Luck

- The business hands have no lines of money or force but could close on Customer of proximity with business and vice versa
- Customer distance can be reduced by advanced loyalty and reward.

Each resourcefulness counts

- But in the global network of users of smart technologies
- Within the cultural context of business changes and markets
- By the overall usability of business products.

You will continue with fat

- In the global bottom line resources and effort that goes along development of Customer pace by business gaps racing in customer care or commitment including inner growth and happiness.

April 3

- Treat yourself as a business fool around the first 3 days of each month for your business credibility and acceptance by all unexpected shocks of market competitors and customers.

Slow and thorough

- Steady decision making process could be helpful to understand that pretext of business to take time to understand the customer to eliminate any extra commitment but not without any concern for time limits.

Control strategy

- Get the grip on Customer worth and hang in there to understand better customer focus than business effort without consulting with customers and employee experiences.

Slippers

- Lagging of Customer understanding not knowing what to ask, seek and expect
- Business is in fix, lurching behind every breakthrough and following user without any involvement with your extra cost.

Advertising is irrationality

- Everything is exaggerated, and every one is lost during the business story recital without being carried away by hypothesis of business and puzzled look of Customer both banking on the unseen, money and understanding.

Rapid response

- Could give customers impression of business fat avoiding details, research and studies
- Can add to confusion if Customer is no clear nor gets new impact
- Is very good if backed by solid reason and novel ideas.

Degenerative business changes

- Competition analysis that is too misguided is not just Business junk but some kind of poison in the long term
- Decoration of Customer in business etiquette rather than product innovation is Hollow fat evading health of business.

Lastly

- Trust your business rationality
- Retain rules of business history
- Usurp competition
- Buy technology and not your tasks

www.ingramcontent.com/pod-product-compliance
Lightning Source LLC
Chambersburg PA
CBHW031444210526
45464CB00005B/2330